Our Side of the Wall

PATRIOTIC AND INSPIRATIONAL POETRY FROM AN UNUSUAL PERSPECTIVE

Our Side of the Wall

PATRIOTIC AND INSPIRATIONAL POETRY FROM AN UNUSUAL PERSPECTIVE

BRIAN B. HAWTHORNE

LitPrime
"Your story is our priority"

LitPrime Solutions
21250 Hawthorne Blvd
Suite 500, Torrance, CA 90503
www.litprime.com
Phone: 1-800-981-9893

Published by LitPrime Solutions   10/17/2022

ISBN: 979-8-88703-061-6(sc)
ISBN: 979-8-88703-062-3(hc)
ISBN: 979-8-88703-063-0(e)

Library of Congress Control Number: 2022917274

Contents

Our Side of the Wall

The souls of heroes are laid down,
Like bricks in ordered rows,
To make a wall, an edifice,
A structure that still grows.

Upon this side, stern silence reigns,
The code of fallen men,
It takes a focused feeling to,
Receive our thoughts again.

The thing that every soldier here,
Would say is short and sweet,
Go live your life but learn as well,
Don't make this scene repeat.

If there were one thing I would say,
I'd say it with a shout!
This wall's not here to keep us in.
It's there to keep you out.

Bobby G. Wells . . . . . May 26, 2008

Someone

He is a regular fellow,
In a place he doesn't belong.
Not that he isn't welcome there,
But the time and place are wrong.

Anger is the morning meal,
For half the local folks,
And fear makes up his breakfast,
Along with nervous jokes.

The weaponry is out there,
And some of it has your name.
Your courage can control your fear,
But rockets don't play that game.

And it's Wham! Bam! Where did that come from?
And fate is looking at me, through the barrel of a gun.
I'm hit! I'm hurt! But I am still alive.
I'm getting myself out of here. Please someone help me drive.

The bomb has landed in me,
It's safe and warm and snug.
I look around at friends of mine.
I know they want to bug.

They take a breath of courage,
And stand to see me through,
I'd like to think that in their place,
That's just what I would do.

The Medic knows the danger,
But he's an angel man.
He knows I'm fighting for my life,
And he'll do what he can.

And it's Wham! Bam! Where did that come from?
And fate is looking at me, through the barrel of a gun.
I'm hit! I'm hurt! But I am still alive.
I'm getting myself out of here. Please someone help me drive.

They rush to get me airborne,
A chance no one should take.
But they are men who stood with me,
They do it for my sake.

Well, some may know I'm married,
A father, gonna be.
But others only see the blood,
And take a chance on me.

I'm no one really special,
No different from the rest,
I guess my only role to play,
Is to put them to the test.

And it's Wham! Bam! Where did that come from?
And fate is looking at me, through the barrel of a gun.
I'm hit! I'm hurt! But I am still alive.
I'm getting myself out of here. Please someone help me drive.

They got me to the clinic.
They got the weapon out.
They took it down the road a piece,
To let it have its shout.

The anger of the world condensed,
Into a blast of rage,
Now safely detonated,
Upon an empty stage.

So all I have to do right now,
Is drag myself along.
And stuff my straw back in my chest,
Get back to being strong.

But it's Wham! Bam! Where did that come from?
And fate is looking at me, through the barrel of a gun.
I'm hit! I'm hurt! But I got through the drive.
Someone got me out of there. Someone kept me alive.

Bobby G. Wells . . . . October 1, 2007

Party Dance

Flowers dance in party dresses,
Insects nuzzle their perfume,
They do this in gardens so that,
We don't have to leave the room.

It isn't birds and bees, you know,
We need to learn about.
These sexy petaled trollops,
Gaily flaunt their wares about.

So shamelessly these hussies,
With color and aroma,
Set out to prove that to succeed,
They'll need no school diploma.

My wife used the weedwhacker,
On bluebells one fine day.
She crashed their jolly party.
I took her tool away.

I forgive their merriment,
Their careless happy airs,
Because at night they bow their heads,
And say their silent prayers.

Bobby G. Wells . . . . . . April 2, 2004

A Walk With God

God and I were walking,
Along the endless sands,
Of the beaches of forever,
On my familiar span.

I had a million questions,
He had one answer, "Yes!"
Whatever's not a small reward,
Is just a simple test.

I try to walk here every day.
We watch the time and tide.
The rhythm of days is lulling,
Just I, and with Him beside.

I have no fear of fortune,
As We are walking here,
For peace and joy encompass me,
Because my God is near.

Bobby G. Wells . . . . April 17, 2007

A Weeping of Stones

This is where the love went, that sang from youthful eyes,
Into the stone which weeps its tears, when joined by weeping skies.
The stone now shouts its lie out, the pain from metal blade,
Here lies the symbol of a love. Here's where the pain has stayed.

The sculptor had an artful eye, and caught the loving glance.
He froze it with a chilling spell, and sundered love's last chance.
Though art could capture what he saw, his heart was dead to sight,
In carving out a lover's stare, he closed off loving's light.

The girl has gone now, her reward, unknown to all of us,
How sad that this reminder then, becomes a warning thus,
Look out upon the world and see the wonder that is there,
But do not close your eye to love, and do not lose your share.

The sculptor died alone, they said, a sad and lonely man,
Who could have found fond happiness, as any of us can.
His fame did not provide for him the pleasures that he'd planned.
But I have seen a face like hers on children of this land.

Bobby G. Wells . . . . November 10, 2004

Among The Dead

Poets tend to take their walks,
Where Angels fear to tread,
Where neither lark nor eagle flew,
And out among the dead.
Gods and monsters congregate,
In places none would dare,
The tallest mountains give a step,
To even thinner air.
With bright illusions he has seen,
The Magic on display,
Where one hand holds a promise up,
The other takes away.
And in the depths of loneliness,
Where songs run out of breath,
With words that whisper truth to all,
The poet threatens Death.

Bobby G. Wells . . . . 27 June, 2012

Home

I've never been far South enough to stand,
Where shadows melt in puddles 'stead of roamin'.
Even when the Sun had journeyed Northward,
It's noontime high still made of me a gnomon.

Not much of a worldwide traveller am I,
I've only traipsed around one continent.
Not that I haven't had the wanderlust,
I think it's safe to blame time management.

Too often I found places, that felt like home to me.
Where hearts could put down roots,
And in the sun, and wind, and rain,
My branches sent out shoots.

So I grew quite attached to them,
And stayed around a while.
And that's why many a year went by,
While I journeyed not a mile.

I do not worry about it,
My travels come to me.
I get a lot of mileage from,
The spinning skies I see.

Turtles and snails have their homes with them,
Whether moving or lying still.
I have my home resting on my back,
As I lie on a grassy hill.

Bobby G. Wells . . . . . . May 23, 2005

I Am Water

I am water. I will flow. There is no place I cannot go.
The heart in darkness still will stop, to taste refreshment in a drop.
Cool liquid, sweet and pure, that brings the strength to help endure.
The conflagration burning near will calm, and cool when I am here.

Descending with my friends who fall as tender mercies come to call.
A message from a Friend on High, arriving when the need is nigh.
I am water. I will seep in arid soil where seeds may sleep.
I'll wake them gently and invite, their rise into the air and light.

My tender touch will gently clean the dust
that falls on leaves of green.
In Nature's garden, I am rain that fills with joy the fruit and grain.
In raging floods of constant thunder, I am that which rips asunder,
The shelters made of stone and sticks that
took your hands so long to fix.

What is my purpose, showing might? Do I oppose you in some fight?
I am that force that breaks the stone, so
plants and flowers can be sown.
I am the hammer blows that fall, to batter down the prison wall,
To make a garden. Food will grow and
gentle souls and hearts may go.

I am water. I am Life. I am joy amid the strife.
Extinguishing the burning blaze, ending droughts, and cutting ways,
Through hardest stone, to break the rocks
and open up the prison locks.
I am water. I am tears. I am with you in your fears.

I will wash your pain away and bring fresh hope at end of day.
I am water. I am you. I will make all things be new.
I am water. I will flow. There is no place I cannot go.
I am the hurts felt as you grow. I am water. I will flow.

Bobby G. Wells . . . . May 1, 2005

Puppets Descending

We are but shadows of puppets,
Descending on strings from above,
From dimensions of will and of timelessness,
And at least one dimension of love.

The long, slow drop takes a lifetime,
But life isn't what we had thought,
Here in the cave of our conscious,
In shadows we find what we've sought.

What we are perceiving as substance,
Is only the shadow poured down,
From an angel writhing in torment,
Descending on strings to the ground.

Expelled from a Presence of glory,
Compelled to a penance below,
The fuzzy outline of the shadow,
Gets sharper as we see it grow.

And the hazy outline of its future,
We see as an infancy here,
Where predictions of ending are valid,
As the shadow's outline grows more clear.

A shadow of many dimensions,
With a substance and weight we perceive,
An illusion convincingly solid,
When the Light is extinguished, will leave.

Our soul doesn't enter when we do,
From birth canals we call alive,
It falls, while we think we're rising,
At the end of the trip it arrives.

And that's when the puppet stops moving,
Having joined with its shadow below,
The delicate dance of descending,
Has made for a marvelous show.

Bobby G. Wells . . . . August 6, 2008

Scarlet Dreams

There is a promise in the sight,
Of redbirds moving 'round in flight.
Their brilliant colors clearly state,
This frozen land is not our fate.

There will be thawing coming soon,
A glacial creeping toward June.
When this bright plumage may seem bland,
As flowers fill a fertile land.

But for the moment all is stark,
A brilliant day turns crisply dark,
And only wind sings mournful dirge,
Of having lost its vernal urge.

Beneath a coverlet of white,
The same bold striving senses night,
And slumbers onward snug in bed,
While scarlet dreams flash overhead.

Bobby G. Wells . . . . January 31, 2005

Shadows

A shadow has two parts, you know.
The one above, the one below.
Within the shadow of a tree,
Toward the light here's what you'll see.

A shaded part of tree is found,
To join the part that's on the ground.
The joining of the two may be,
Inseparable, like ground and tree.

But as the world turns through the day,
The shadow starts upon its way.
To join its cousins in the night,
And leave the clinging one in fright.

The world has turned its face away,
From that bright light that we call day.
The darkness that befalls thereon.
Will stay until the break of dawn.

The night is shadow's fearful half,
The other part leaps with a laugh,
Out where it dwindles to a dot,
Evaporating on the spot,

Unless the moon has ventured in,
As round the Earth it does its spin.
The shadow is a twin at birth,
Even when its mother's Earth.

With one that clings close to its mother,
And one that flies away from brother.
Its journey's length always depends,
On what befalls before it ends.

Bobby G. Wells . . . . March 3, 2004

Second Stage

Rockets don't keep going up. They reach a zenith in their flight,
And then the second stage starts up, and takes them out of sight.
I've zoomed up from the surface and I've reached the highest part,
Now's the time the second stage should have its start,

To carry me more Heavenward than is my heart's desire,
I'm waiting for that second stage to catch its fire.
I'll wave Good-Bye to all of you as I'm propelled aloft,
While laughing at the ones who shook
their heads and grimly scoffed.

Acceleration will pull back my lips into a rictus grin,
My smile will let you see I know just what I'm getting in.
That second stage will carry me up to my Heaven's Gate.
I hope the timing is set right, don't want to get there late.

And so I'm sitting here just waiting for that second stage to fire,
Without it, it is sure that I will never get much higher,
I'm sitting here and looking round, and wondering somehow,
It should be starting up real soon, like right about now.

Like right about now.

Like right about now.

Bobby G. Wells . . . . February 2, 2006

Sharing

I did not know I thirsted, before you brought me drink.
A world of hidden, secret thoughts, was all that I could think.
The bread of your companionship has filled me to the core,
And now I think I understand what friendship is here for.

My world was one of loneliness. Am I the only one?
But with your cheery friendship, I learned there could be fun.
I cast my seeds in wider ways than I have ever known,
And send the net out presently, to draw in what I've sown.

My world has grown, and joy has found a way to get inside.
I had no thought that I would find the world become my bride.
My heart has also swelled in scope, a garden lives there now.
And all these things occurred to me, because of you, somehow.

My friends who touch me with their words, can reach into my heart,
And find a way to thrill my soul, that I've become a part,
Of something bigger than myself, a movement grand and slow,
More ponderous and possible than what I thought I'd know.

Bobby G. Wells . . . . April 10, 2005

18

Solace

"How are things?" They say to me.
A pleasant friendly inquiry.
How can I tell them how I feel?
They did not know my dream was real.

They thought I seemed content until,
A sadness flooded in to fill,
This heart that you had dwelled inside,
And warmed me in the eventide.

They think that with you gone that I,
Can not find solace though I try.
That with an emptiness in me,
There is no room for ecstasy.

A hollow space would fill me up,
Prevent my drinking from the cup?
How can they think that you would go,
And not remain inside me so?

That you are with me even now,
Your hand in mine as we did vow.
We could not ever come apart,
Because we share each other's heart.

Your laughter rings in silent rooms,
That others think are soundless tombs.
Your smile can brighten every day.
How can they think you've gone away?

My father walks beside me still,
He gives advice, and always will.
My mother sings as she once did,
When lifting up the stewpot's lid.

The life she spent in serving others,
She gently nurtured in my brothers.
Indeed in all who came around,
Each came to find what she had found.

That life alone is but a seed,
Incapable of worthy deed.
But when the light of love shines in,
The roots take hold, the vines to spin,

Entangling all in matted grip,
That even death can not make slip.
The raindrop tears of daily woes,
Are soaked up in the childlike toes.

And winds of passion and of fear,
Which bring destruction circling near,
Are but the welcome cleansing breeze,
To wash the dust from sturdy trees.

No, I am never quite alone.
I'm filled inside with thoughts my own,
Of days spent laughing, having fun,
Relaxing when our work was done.

They see me smile and think that I,
Just reminisce of days gone by.
They cannot know I feel more joy,
Than when I was a little boy.

I knew not then that pain could hurt,
I didn't know that girls could flirt,
There was a world I couldn't see,
And now it lives inside of me.

My struggle now is just to show,
The happiness I've come to know.
How can I share with them this thrill?
The ones I love are with me still.

Bobby G. Wells . . . . . March 1, 2004

The Glass Half Full

Each of us is a vessel,
Upwelling with life and with joy,
In childhood you see this bubblingness,
So delightful in each girl and boy.

Somewhere someone noticed,
Philosopher type, I would guess,
That some of us see a glass half full,
And some of us see it as less.

We've noticed that life can be short, sometimes,
We're hurt if it happens to be,
But it is only the vessel that comes up short,
The life is unending, you see.

We slake our thirst from a fountain,
That flows for all of our days,
And none of us ever is half filled up,
Our cup runneth over, always.

Bobby G. Wells . . . June 30, 2010

The Heart is a Fist-Sized Organ

The heart is a fist-sized organ,
That works throughout the day,
It clenches and throbs with a rhythm,
And it hasn't much time for play.

Our hearts have grown used to grabbing,
And holding on for dear life,
It's hard to know that we must relax,
Amid all the tumult and strife.

The music it beats to is distant,
In quiet we hear it the best,
That's when we stop all the straining,
And that's when the heart takes a rest.

It isn't just muscle that does the work,
But a cycle, (I thought you might ask!),
Like an oar lifted out of the water,
That then bends once again to the task.

In order to function as it's designed,
It must squeeze a bit, and then let go,
And just like the times of excitement,
It can race, or it can go slow.

Our loved ones enter to fill us,
They empty us when they must leave,
Oh, what a hurtful happiness!
The sad joy that compels us to grieve.

Cupid's arrows are just tiny wedges,
Finding chinks in the armor to slip,
To batter the stony exterior,
With a lifetime to loosen the grip.

Like a hand that can clench or be gentle,
Now held open to something above.
The heart is a fist-sized organ,
That's receiving an inflow of love.

Bobby G. Wells . . . . . . December 8, 2006

The Cabin Window

No matter how rude the cabin,
The window will face to the scene,
Of Winter's fresh carpet of glory,
Or Summer's lush meadow of green.

The window's a part of the inside,
It makes the insidedness right.
For it shows what you're trying to keep away,
The storms, and the bumps in the night!

Like a magnet that has both a north and a south,
Our comforts align the same way.
While you stare at your pleasant warm fire,
The window will show the cold day.

For while your feet are in slippers,
As you snuggle down all of your toes,
The window displays the rain and the wind,
As a lullaby helping you doze.

Bobby G. Wells . . . . . . December 4, 2006

Rain

Rain refreshes. Rain rewards.
Kills our thirst with liquid swords.
Washes all the dust away,
And bends the light at end of day.

Rain helps soothe us into sleep,
Cleans up the world we're sworn to keep.
We tend to it, and it to us,
We're well rewarded for the fuss.

Like magic mushrooms popping up,
Our food shows in the flowing cup,
A horn of plenty, our reward,
And liquid coolness from the gourd.

Rain comes by to cool our brow,
To give a rest from labors now,
While forces sent from up above,
Gently whisper, "Here's the Love!"

Bobby G. Wells . . . . . Sept. 24, 2006

Why Have I Been Weeping?

I see the faces in the park, and each one tells a story,
Some bitter from the striving, some faded with their glory.
Some look out on the park and see the life inside them,
And some have hurts upon their face with nowhere else to hide them.

A comely matron passes by, her pride protects her pain,
She doesn't seem to notice that her smile is showing strain.
A pair of schoolgirls next are seen, and giggle as they pass,
I hope their laughter will grow up when laddy meets his lass.

An old man sits near dozing with the sun upon his face,
I know that in his mind he is no longer near this place.
Instead he walks with hand about the love that he once held,
And now he sits with frozen smile where happiness has gelled.

A woman looks into my eyes, a question seems to rise,
Although her lips say nothing it is clearly in her eyes.
"Oh, stranger, do you know the pain I'm feeling in my heart?
Can you tell why I've been weeping? Do
you know what made me start?"

I only know the answer to a question still unasked,
For it is the answer always for the way we have been tasked.
The answer is to love someone, though someone brought you pain,
Even though you're hurting now, you still must love again.

For love is still the answer to the way to get through life,
And it doesn't matter if you fail, or if you live in strife.
You must share your pain and loneliness, and laugh it all away,
And you'll find that pain is ebbing as love's tide flows in today.

Step out of the shadow of the pain that brought you grief,
And hold a child, and see her smile, and you will feel relief.
No matter how you're hurting, and no matter what you've lost,
There's even more to be received, with negligible cost.

Your life has many turnings, at the end you may look back,
And though you know you lost something,
there's nothing that you lack.
The life that seemed so shattered has been made into a whole,
And your audience applauds you for your stunning, starring role.

Bobby G. Wells . . . . April 19, 2004

With My Shield, Or On It

I know it is upsetting,
To see things done this way.
Flag-draped caskets side by side,
They're headed home today.

One thing you might not think about,
The view from the inside.
I've got some time now on my hands,
While on this final ride.

Sorry I didn't write more,
Too late to fix that now.
I'll try to be more scrupulous,
To get word out somehow.

There are no easy channels,
But I'm sure that you will know,
I don't regret the choice I made,
And why I had to go.

You'd think perhaps the view from here,
Would be quite dark inside,
But it is light as light can be,
My burden's been untied.

And I've been lifted up,
On angel wings I think,
And I've got every thing I need,
Except our kitchen sink.

I'd like to wash my hands once more,
And turn and get a hug.
I wish I could shake the hand of,
My best friend too, ya lug.

But all that stuff is over now,
I've got my new assignment,
Looks like I hitched my wagon to,
A different star alignment.

I know I always promised Mom,
I'd try to be real good,
Will someone please just let her know,
I did the best I could.

I have to go now, duty calls,
Think of me when you can,
The folks will think they lost their boy,
My buddies saw a man.

Bobby G. Wells . . . April 25, 2004

You Watch The Moon

You speak of moonlight, while I sweat,
Your evening hasn't got here yet.
The moon you see, will shine for me,
As I lie down with memory,

My worries, and the day's heartaches,
And all the pain from my mistakes.
I gather calmness from the dusk,
And breathe the scents of evening's musk,

The twilight brings the evening's calm,
And confidence from your song's balm.
For you have seen this day and night,
And found it not a source for fright.

You faced the challenge, and in time,
Incorporated it in rhyme.
You walked with Day and held its hand,
While you stood strong in a foreign land.

The heart of evil that will try,
To harm us must first face your eye,
And you will cause its force to wither,
Before it dares to journey hither.

We thank you then for standing there,
While we sleep soundly without care.
Your loved ones and a grateful nation,
Protected from War's desolation,

A world away, but held so close,
Each of us missing what we love most.
Take heart that as you watch the moon,
Your task will end, you'll come home soon.

Bobby G. Wells . . . . March 27, 2005

"Why Is Your Face
So Wrinkled, Grandma?"

When I was born, my children's child,
I was with stone at heart.
No joy or laughter did exist,
To penetrate my dark.

I watched a gray world petrify,
As green and blue turned gray,
And summer sunshine led to night,
While warm hands went away.

And so, stone statue that I was,
I looked up at the sky,
While passing clouds I dimly saw,
Rained down to help me cry.

So slowly, slowly did my face,
Dissolve and wash away,
Til now my ruined visage looks without,
As in, in younger days.

These fissures and the furrows deep,
Are now my map of peace,
Those students of my journey long,
Know soon I'll find surcease.

But only for a moment now,
I hold a child and see,
Unwrinkled planes of bright desire,
Fond hope that once was me.

Bobby G. Wells . . . . February 16, 2008

Gnarled

The hands reach out, once more again,
Adept at dealing with tasks at hand.
Gnarled, and twisted, but so strong,
And used to setting right what's wrong.

Could he have been a surgeon? No,
Though dextrous, these fingers were not so,
With delicate strength of fine control,
And subtle movements in a larger whole.

His were the hands that swung a pick,
Or axe, and metal tools held by a stick,
The swinging arm, the muscles bunched,
No music from the things he crunched.

He beat the world down all around,
To make his place, and stand his ground.
No task was easy from his birth,
His was a world of stubborn earth.

And yet, in gross examples of his art,
He showed the love deep in his heart.
His strength was guided in its course,
By limits to the use of force.

And when the oak was split, and planed,
He felt the smoothness that he'd gained.
Removing roughness was his art,
He practiced it upon his heart.

He could have held a wolf at bay,
And yet I well recall the day,
His little dog was taken ill,
The tears from every eye did spill.

And though his strength was that of ten,
He could not work his magic then,
No tools he had would fill the bill,
His gnarled and twisted hands lay still.

The roughness of the world struck back,
And proved that it could still attack.
How like a splinter one small pet,
Will not allow one to forget.

His work is done now, his hands rest.
It's now my turn to pass the test.
I've set out on my own grand quest.
His work is done now. His hands rest.

NicknamedBob . . . . February 20, 2005

From The Cave

We stare morosely at the rain,
As we sit in the mouth of the den.
There'll be no game to flush,
No tracks to smell, so then ...

It's back into the labyrinth,
Where darkened comfort waits,
And soon enough, a meal appears,
On clean and shiny plates.

The animals who live here,
Accommodate our pack,
For we stand guard, protecting them,
That's how we pay them back.

Bobby G. Wells . . . . October 26, 2007

Fog Flowers

I like to call them Fog Flowers, those tiny crystals of rain.
They carpet the world in silence, they glorify dirt in the lane.
There seems all a hush to their presence, the softest tinkle of sound,
And even the animals quiet, as a blanket descends on the town.

Some look upon it as frigid, but warming and soft is the throw,
The flowers asleep in the garden, will snuggle and smile under snow.
"But it makes the road too slippery!" I hear
the complaints starting now.
As it furrows and windblows and softens, the
marks that were left by the plow.

You seem to not understand it, this miracle silently wrought.
For where will you go now to find it, when
this is what you have sought?
A promise of hope from your Father, a gentle reminder of love,
Each entity fallen from Heaven, is getting a kiss from above.

Bobby G. Wells . . . . December 5, 2004

From The Not So Blue

Some days, like a bolt from the blue, or from the not so blue,
You're struck by something powerful, something that is true.
Unassailable recognition, of power and of strength,
That tends to tilt the world you view, and makes you think at length.

What is the purpose of our lives? What do we struggle for?
Do we wander an aimless thicket, or is there a Golden Door?
You can be sitting at a desk, or riding in a car,
When suddenly you're somewhere else,
though you haven't gone so far.

Epiphanies can happen. They do not have to hurt.
You think you're full of love for life, and then you have dessert!
Our lives are a rich conundrum, some things we know or guess,
But when you can have a gift from on high,
you should always answer Yes!

Bobby G. Wells . . . . May 20, 2005

Grounded!

Bernice was just a worker bee,
But she did love her work.
She loved to smell the flowers,
And never did she shirk.

She found a good patch one fine day,
Began to gather nectar,
She filled up all her pockets,
And noted well the vector.

She'd need to pass the word along,
She'd do the "waggle-dance",
But she was really weighted down.
She might not get the chance!

With all the weight she carried,
She glided to the ground.
She couldn't fly another inch,
She'd have to walk around.

She trudged all through the morning,
Quite sure that she would swoon.
She trekked onward valiantly,
Til it was half past Noon.

With her forepaws held around her mouth,
As if they were a cup,
She shouted "Help!" to those above,
"I've pollen, and I can't get up!"

Bobby G. Wells . . . October 14, 2004

When All Is Sad And Dun

When all is sad and dun,
And all my days have run,
Up to the ending point,

I'll look about and think,
Now that I'm on the brink,
Just why was I in this joint?

I don't recall the invite,
Or where I spent last night,
But this has been a fine place for the run.

Though now that I am older,
The nights are growing colder,
And even days are awfully sad and dun.

Bobby G. Wells . . . . May 31, 2008

We Saved A Seat

We keep a place in the parlor, a seat for an old friend,
Someone who went to fight for us, we shall not see again.
But just in case he wanders by, he's welcome to a rest.
We've got the seat saved just for him, as flowers will attest.

We don't expect to see him, though we think of him a lot.
We only know he said, "I'm going, and I'll give it all I've got."
We know he gave it that and more, and didn't pass in vain.
I guess we sorta knew it when he stepped up on the train.

I'd rather think of him that way, instead of in the mud.
And certainly I wouldn't want to think about the blood.
Determined was his visage, and noble was his cause,
And when we count our blessings 'round, we stop here and we pause.

Bobby G. Wells . . . . May 3, 2004

Ash Dream

Sometimes, in a fireplace, a limb will be consumed,
So slowly, so gently, that it retains its form,
Just as it was in life; the shape of the veins,
The mark of the bark. It shares those moments warm,

And filled with sunshine, having knitted structure,
Out of the very air. Such magic! -- that it weaves its dreams,
In daylight, making sugar chains too long for eating,
For any but termites, or beavers by their streams.

Those streams of tears that fell upon the hills,
After traveling on the sighs of tropic wistfulness,
To dash out all their hopes in Northern climes,
For trees to sip, and gossip with a stately cheerfulness.

And so this ashen ghost of form, observed by dreamers,
Resembles what we think we may become one day,
When all our cheerful sunniness, our hopes and dreams,
Have spun and scattered forth like Autumn leaves at play.

Perhaps one day I will be sitting in a park,
With wistful smiles recalled upon my face,
Having become an ashen image of my self,
That scatters to the winds without a trace.

Bobby G. Wells . . . . November 29, 2008

A Thank You Note

That was such a lovely thought,
I think I'll write to say,
"Your work was inspirational,
It helped me through the day!"
But then I think, No, let it go,
It seems a sappy thing,
Let someone else communicate,
I don't have much to bring.
The one who gave this thing to me,
Won't worry how I feel,
Another day I'll put words down,
So that they know it's real.
And so procrastination,
An enemy of grace,
Makes silent our compassion,
Applause seems out of place.
The giver then must wonder,
Did I offend somehow?
I haven't heard a single word,
What could have gone wrong now?
When you are moved to thank someone,
Don't hesitate at all,
The soul that feels the pulse of life,
Seems quick to have a fall.
Just think of the young artists,
The sadness that you face,
To learn another voice has stilled,
And silence took its place.
Who knows to what degree a note,
Of thankfulness would make?

Kind words can sometimes fill the thirst,
That other things might slake.
And if these souls are needing,
Appreciation's glow,
What of the One who gave us all,
That we have come to know?
As you go through your busy life,
Take time throughout the day,
To say, "You've done some classic work,
"That's all I have to say."

Bobby G. Wells . . . . April 2, 2004

A Mother Is ...

A mother is a messenger, who bears a precious gift,
And even in the wrapping we can find some gems to sift.
The more we learn of life, the more we stop and stare,
For how can such a wondrous thing be conjured out of air?

A mother is a vessel, a type of cooking pot,
Whose love provides the warmth so that it doesn't get too hot.
And she provides the nutrients, our flesh is of her soil,
And when the child is born it's she who does the toil,

Of cleaning it, and feeding it, and teaching it to smile,
A small reward to mother for her efforts all the while.
A mother is a garden spot, where God instills a spark,
A holy flame to kindle for the world's encroaching dark.

For every child's a candle, sent to fill the world with light,
And mother is the shielded hand that saves it for the night.
A mother does the work of God in bringing forth a child,
And Godly patience helps her to prevent its running wild.

We recognize her efforts with some flowers and a card,
Oblivious to the challenges she faced, and it was hard,
To make a sterling citizen from the plans placed in her head,
She had to compromise a bit, 'cause she got us instead.

Bobby G. Wells . . . . May 8, 2004

Album Pages

The sky was milky blue, with clouds of perfect white,
I knew that it would gently fade, into a misty night.
A day of quaint perfection, to steep our memories,
Of laughter, hands in hands, and smiling in the breeze.

I always love a perfect day. I gather all I can.
Sometimes I have to bend the rules, to make them fit my plan.
A little bit of rain is not a killer of the day.
And splashing through the puddles is a way to make it play.

Even snow can sometimes be a pleasure to enfold,
Perfection isn't measured by the heat or by the cold.
It's measured by the moments that are strung up just like pearls,
As are the gilded seconds that young men enjoy with girls.

Every day's an album page with images to hold.
The sunshine seems much brighter, and the colors much more bold.
We turn the page with sadness til we get a chance to look,
Back upon the memories we cherish in our book.

Bobby G. Wells . . . . July 1, 2004

At Sunset

Every day at Sunset, the Angels spill their paint,
Across the largest canvas, and work without complaint.

Although few eyes are watching, and light is fading fast,
They create a marvelous portrait, as if it were going to last.

But this beauty is so fleeting, you have to watch it grow,

And when the light is gone at last,

. . . it will leave you with a glow.

Bobby G. Wells . . . . . Sept 2, 1999

Being A Kid

Being a kid means never having to say you're sorry, and mean it!
It means someone will come along and fix it, you can play.
It means that tiny things can mean a lot to you, a marble, or a peanut,
And you will get to eat, before your stomach says, "Okay!"

And someone will remind you that you need to sleep.

It means you know someone who always has the money,
To operate the candy vending thing, and will.
But makes you do those silly things like ask,
And won't cooperate with voices that are shrill.

Someone who thinks a promise is to keep.

It means that all you ever have to do is play,
'Cause that's the way you learn things, don't you know?
And they will praise you for the funny things you say,
Unless you got them staying up to watch a show!

And they'll carry you uphill when it is steep.

Bobby G. Wells . . . . July 8, 2005

Behold, I Stand
at the Door

Here in this world there's a chance.
Opportunity comes each day,
To turn around our lives and live
In that exemplary way.

I've known about the doorway,
My parents knocked me too.
There isn't any question that,
I know what I should do.

But here is what concerns me,
Let's call it Heaven's Key,
"The only way to the Kingdom,"
(His words!) "… is by me."

So the crux of my dilemma,
Believe me, it's a gem.
If I have blocked His way down here,
How can I get by Him?

Bobby G. Wells . . . . August 12, 2007

At Bottom

They brought some new stock in today,
And dumped it on my head!
"You have to rotate stock, you know!"
Was what I should have said.

Instead I suffered silently,
I've done that far too long.
One needs to speak up fervently,
When something's clearly wrong!

It's such a simple job, I thought,
I'll get a chance to shine!
The other apples all around,
I think would rather whine.

They've clearly lost ambition,
Can't do the simplest task.
Just suck it up and hold it in,
Is that too much to ask?

I guess a case of attitude,
Is what I now have gotten,
From too much pressure felt too long.
Boy, do I feel rotten.

Bobby G. Wells . . . . July 26, 2005

Before There Was Dirt

When I was a little kid, a real long time ago,
We didn't have a lot of things that you have come to know.
There was no clothing fashion, because no one wore clothes,
We spent our time just looking 'round, and saying, "Look at those!"

A boy without a pocket means a boy without a frog.
We had a sort of clubhouse. We called our place "the log."
The grown-ups never scolded us, we didn't have the words.
I got a lot of credit then, for coming up with "birds."

We summered in a place they called the briddish isles,
The briddish folk who lived up there seemed generous with smiles.
The little hopping critters that had grown their feathers out,
Seemed happy, so I called them brids, a word that went about.

The word got twisted round a bit, and so it came out bird,
But we were very language poor and needed our new word.
The job of giving names to things was one for senior folk,
And I was so much younger then, they took it as a joke.

But still the word got out and I got better known,
And in a way because of it, I got one of my own.
They gave me tufts of feathers, and tied them in a knot,
A rumper-sticker that said Bird-On-Board was something else I got.

After a while just B-O-B was stuck upon my rear,
And when I left somewhere they said BOB has been here.
We traveled around the world back then, or what we knew of it,
Some places seemed to be real nice, and some we quickly split.

There was one place that many thought was very fine and grand,
They dug their caves in nice soft rock, it was a holey land.
The sun shone down too brightly there, some guys became a pain,
Or maybe it was something else that drove the folks insane.

There was a kid who lived down there who played a game on sand,
His hoard of aggies proved he was the best one in the land.
Methuselah, he called himself, and challenged me to play,
I could afford to lose a few, and think I made his day.

I haven't seen him lately. I think he may be gone.
Young kids like him could never seem to keep their britches on.
It wasn't that he seemed to be the nervous type,
He just needed to be patient, and then to get more ripe.

I used to like a place that was a little North of there,
We still had warmer weather, and breezes filled the air.
A peaceful fishing village, somewhere they broke a dam,
We left some really bad words there when we went on the lam.

And so we wandered on a bit and learned to cope with life.
I grew somewhat stronger when I first encountered strife.
It was the prudent thing to do, to turn the other cheek,
One cheek too many though, could mean that you were weak.

I learned how to handle, those ones who'd be my foe,
It wouldn't do to travel on, with nowhere left to go.
You make a man respect you, and he can be your friend,
And if he cannot live with that, you bring it to an end.

On the whole I'm peaceful, and settled in my ways,
And I didn't really hanker for the more exciting days.
So I stayed pretty busy, avoiding getting hurt,
And life was pretty good to me, before we dealt with dirt.

Life was so much cleaner then, before the dirt arrived,
We strolled about the planet. Our numbers grew. We thrived.
We didn't have much in the way of automatic toys,
But we had girls to chase, and they had all us boys.

And so our numbers went on up, more people every day,
The "planning" folks were not around to interfere that way.
Some had funny notions, and lived the way they wished.
Others took it easy. They hunted and they fished.

The animals around us seemed to give us lots of room,
Except for certain hungry ones, and meeting them was doom.
Some of us didn't like that. We set out to fix their wagon.
We came back wearing nice warm skins. The others left, tails draggin'.

Without the dirt, we didn't know, about the bathing reason,
We thought the little odors were, someone was not in season.
The animals didn't look on us in "fawning" admiration,
They actually avoided us with our protective odoration.

It took a long time to discover which ideas beat the others,
Some folks lived on other's work. Most treated men like brothers.
In the marketplace of thought, many notions came to flower,
And you never knew which one would be the flavor of the hour.

We all had lots of time to sit around and think,
My suggestions fell quite flat, because like me, they'd stink.
But I got better as I went, and sometimes had a thought,
That could have saved us trouble if the others would have bought.

My plan for building Stonehenge was to make it as a star,
With North and South along a line that went so far,
And lines to mark the point to which the sun would make its way,
In Winter's slow migration up until the shortest day.

Too bad the guy in charge did not see things my way,
Or folks would not be looking on, and scratching heads today.
But he insisted circular, and folks began the work,
My stellar plans were set aside. He was a circle jerk.

I left that merry England, and others left there too,
It wasn't all so merry then, too many folks were blue.
The pyramids were much more fun, the competition brisk,
We raced those stones on up the ramps and didn't mind the risk.

I laugh to think about the thoughts that we used "rays."
Life was so much simpler then, it's how we filled our days,
With building competitions, instead of fighting wars,
Why else would we pile up stones, without a trace of doors?

We'd clap an arc of wood upon each face of cubic block,
And then we'd get it up to go, by pushing up the rock.
Then toss a rope around it, and take it for a stroll,
Let me tell you, we knew then, just how to rock and roll.

Someone asked of getting sick. We had a simple plan.
My way of dealing with it was, avoid it if you can.
If you called attention to yourself, when feeling ill one day,
Others would take notice soon, and go the other way.

It wasn't a matter of cowardice, or feeling no remorse,
It's just that lacking training, there was no other course.
The wisdom of the action, can still be proved today,
For how could AIDS be what it is, if folks weren't turned wrong-way?

Political correctness, was not so big a deal,
We knew it wasn't only wrong, we knew it wasn't real.
When you reward someone, for doing something dumb,
You just create a person who'll be nothing but a bum.

The old ways were not always the best way to abide,
But we learned before we threw them out, to set them side-by-side,
Before we tossed out customs, where errors may have lurked,
We tested them to see results, and find which system worked.

So when did dirt arrive? I guess you ought to know,
It's been a thing that's bugging me, since oh so long ago.
It was the stupid insects, those little robot bums,
"They'll do the work of twenty men, and all of it for crumbs."

Another bright idea, at least it wasn't mine,
The first designs were clever, and seemed to work out fine.
But when the bug got busted up, it wouldn't go away,
Instead the parts got smaller, and turned the dust to gray.

And every time you'd smack one down, or step upon a few,
You'd find a nasty substance, encrusted on your shoe.
You think they get recycled? Just trust me when I say,
The very first bug ever made, you're walking on today.

The knowledge of unmaking them was limited to few,
The scrolls at Alexandria told us just what we should do,
So naturally, disaster fell, and no one knew quite why,
But I can tell you this, it was some stupid firefly.

I miss those simpler times when we all could get along,
We had our bread and wine, and in the evening, we had song.
Our musical devices could plunk out a pretty tune,
And more personal fulfillment could be found behind a dune.

But every day since I've been born has been a joy to me,
And I still get real excited with each new thing that I see.
I've still got time ahead of me and I've worked out all the math,
And I've even gotten used to knowing when to take a bath.

Bobby G. Wells . . . . Feb 28 -- March 2, 2004

Between

Between the dreams and the waking,
As dawn comes up in the land,
There comes a moment of clarity,
That I feel I could touch with my hand.

I can know that I'm no longer dreaming,
But my mind doesn't say that it's wrong,
That the dream-stuff still may linger,
The way music trails off in a song.

So at that moment's perception,
As I rise quite refreshed from my rest,
I form up a flower of loveliness,
To remind me of how I've been blessed.

Then as the long day develops,
While dealing with folks and their schemes,
I lower my head for a moment,
To breathe from the flower I dreamed.

Bobby G. Wells . . . . . . August 8, 2008

Blue Against The Gray

The battle rages onward; the Blue against the Gray!
No one can tell which side will be triumphant on this day!
For Blue was in ascendancy, when morning light arose,
But Gray has come a-gathering, and stands in silent rows.

The darkening skies brood menacingly, and evil seems afoot,
While all the azure bands have let their marching orders put,
Safe distance from the nemesis. They leave the field in haste.
No need before these numbers for their purity to waste.

Behold a view of constant Gray from East across to West,
No red is seen within the bands, and so, perhaps that's best.
The Gray encampment settles in, and rain begins to fall.
No Blue is seen for miles around as if beyond a wall.

As darkness comes some light appears in flashes from the camp,
A sodden night of misery awash in constant damp.
By morning it has spent itself, and in the dark of night,
The Gray has slipped in silence from the field without a fight.

Beyond the hill appears the first of radiant Blue and Gold,
The army of the future guarantees it will unfold,
A calm and brilliant day unfurls as if emerging from a dream,
As sunshine bakes the moisture from the hill in wisps of steam.

The Blue will win the day today, but just before the night,
The clouds of disguised Grays will rise, like ships hove into sight,
And yet another battle from horizon to its brother,
Will silently unfold just as one day becomes another.

The Blues and Grays must struggle on forever, so it seems.
As sunshine burns the steam that falls as tears into the streams,
And weary crowds of stumbling ghosts trek onward as they must,
Until the last sad witness has surrendered to the dust.

Bobby G. Wells . . . . January 25, 2006

Bridges

Bridges are wrinkles along the road,
Where troubles might sully our feet.
Don't want to dampen our spirits,
In our progress along the street.

Most of them cover rivers,
Or rivulets, streams, and the like,
Which means that they've come from upriver,
Where the tears of sad clouds came to strike.

For clouds are conveyors of sadness,
Transporting warm tears on the fly,
Lifting some spirits as they move along,
To the head-water hills where they cry.

And all of these gathered droplets,
Together can make a real force,
Tearing down the mountainsides,
As they rush about in their course.

The water in all of our rivers,
Was carried aloft in a cloud,
They represent distant sadness,
Perhaps from a dream not allowed.

So, just as the children tell you,
As you rise on the bridge from your street,
Lift up your legs in the crossing,
Don't let them dampen your feet.

Bobby G. Wells . . . . November 22, 2007

When Nature is
the Sculptor...

"When nature is the sculptor," you get surprising art.
For she excels at fitting in, and balance plays a part.
Sometimes you'll see things multiplied, to four or even five.
But at its core you'll always find, a pair keeps it alive.

You'll never find a single thing, those unicorns are rare.
For nature likes things doubled up, there's strength in hiding there.
A thing alone will not last long, it seeks to find another,
In all the world it will be lost, if it can't find its brother.

Nature doesn't care, you see, about those strange proportions.
If there's a niche to fill, it will, no matter the contortions.
For that is how we got giraffe, and hippopotami,
And hummingbirds, and butterflies, and duck-billed platypi.

Nature doesn't care about what we call beautiful.
For all she needs is something that is not impossible.
We'll round the edges off in future generations,
Until they're so successful they will be our new sensations.

And has nature had a hand in what we see as so befitting?
I think we would be stranger still if we had done the knitting.
For why do we have hair up there and not defensive horn?
And why not have a tail with us to be our prickling thorn?

If we had been in charge of what we all have come to be,
I think it's clear that all will have to see what I can see.
Our choices would have changed us into quite a frightful show,
Whatever kept us from this path? The Devil if I know!

Bobby G. Wells . . . . February 22, 2004

Last Fall

The days are short, the wind has grown,
My community has now all flown.
I stare at emptiness all around,
And brownish carpeting on the ground.

When I was young, so long ago,
The days seemed endless, ever so.
I was so green. I've learned a lot.
So many shared my lofty spot.

We danced and twirled the time away,
Forgetful of the length of day,
With unseen music through the bright,
And whispers in the silent night.

Alone, I watch the neighborhood,
A stark and silent stretch of wood,
Tears sometimes dim the golden days,
Until the scene is filled with haze.

And only memory serves to fill,
The lonely times upon this hill.
They all have gone now, I remain,
A sad perspective is my gain.

They've departed, this way and that,
A graceful tip of an invisible hat,
And scattered to the winds they were,
Until only I am left to stir,

I twist to shed the Winter's blast,
As I enjoy my being last,
And in the bleak and dismal scene,
I long for days when things were green.

One morning, I awake to find,
The world transformed while I was blind.
In darkness, change had come within the night,
The brown became a world of white!

In joy at last I chanced the breeze,
And danced among the stark black trees.
On stiffened fingertips, I race,
Across the snow without a trace.

All through the day I dance and twirl,
'Til dizzy with the endless whirl,
I fetch up in a tent of green,
And on a sturdy trunk I lean.

The needle-leaves fresh fragrance sends,
With frozen tears the branch then bends.
I look at stars through crystal lens,
I settle down, and dream of friends.

Bobby G. Wells . . . . . October 19, 2006

World Class

Pirouetting ballerina, too rotund for this, her role,
Twirling, tilting, wobbling, is she really in control?
Her attendant, circling 'round her, jumping at her every lurch,
Turns his face as if to worship this bright candle of his church.

Spotlight brilliant, lighting poor, choreography refined,
Twirling round her is her garment, cloak of ebon, silken-lined.
Garish make-up in the footlight, sweatdrops where it's not so bright,
In the darkness of her shadow, glistened shimmers catch the light.

Unheard music guides her movement, Holst
could hear what she perceives,
Circling to the stage-front closely, then so far you'll think she leaves.
Far back curtains hang in velvet, dusted with some sequined art.
Please hold your applause for later, what you've seen is just a start!

Bobby G. Wells . . . . August 8, 2005

Long Walk Day

Olduvai Gorge was a long time ago. We've
walked for quite a long way.
We've picked up things as we walked about,
some habits seem likely to stay.
We've learned to stay together, protecting each other from harm,
The father defending his children, as long
as there's strength in his arm.

The mothers will tend to their hurtings,
and cuddle them up in the cold.
The healthy lend strength to weaker ones,
and patiently stand with the old.
We've gotten to places so hidden away that
you had to be born there to find,
And we learned the hard lessons and followed the
rules, and we keep them firmly in mind.

Our strength is in our joining, our glue the words we share,
All journeys may have some reward,
coming home's beyond compare.
Our eyes may be looking outward, our heart is in the home,
And when we find the truth of that, there is no need to roam.

Bobby G. Wells . . . . October 5, 2004

Life Is Like A Caravan

Life is like a caravan,
Crossing the desert sea,
And being a tiny animal,
That some of you call a flea.

My name is actually Reuben,
But it's all a matter of taste,
I know that most of you do eat meat,
And most of it's left to waste.

I only nibble a little,
I don't really do any harm,
Environmental activists,
Act like I've chewed off an arm.

But camels don't have arms, you know.
They're just a leggy lump,
Life is like a caravan,
And tomorrow I go over the Hump.

Bobby G. Wells . . . March 28, 2006

Lost In Macy's

I got lost in Macy's,
So I went to the Lost and Found.
I thought I could be found in there,
But no one was around.

I sat down to wait a bit,
Among things that people lose,
I snuggled down in soft stuffed toys,
And took a little snooze.

Later, when I woke myself,
The store had gotten dark.
I have to say it had me scared!
Like a cemetery park.

I sneaked off then to the bathroom,
And kept my head down low.
The mannequins were scary, still,
Their shadows made a show.

I couldn't figure why my folks,
Just chose to leave me there.
Weren't they worried about me?
Didn't they even care?

I knew that I would find them,
They wouldn't travel far.
Although they had my money,
I had to drive the car.

Bobby G. Wells . . . . . March 12, 2005

A Well Of Joy

There is a well of joy in you,
An ocean in your blood.
Be glad for this component,
The rest of you is mud.

Deep down inside your spirit,
A depth of strength and love,
Wells up to bring the zest to life,
A gift from up above.

When parched by circumstances,
Or reeling from a blow,
Tap into depths of energy,
Unlimited below.

The lifting of this resource,
Will lift you up as well,
To slake your thirst for happiness,
In places that you dwell.

The desert land of loneliness,
The mountains of despair,
Are quite improved by tiny sips,
Of nectar you can share.

Just reach inside your spirit,
The recipe is this,
When desolation comes to call,
Give it a sloppy kiss!

Bobby G. Wells . . . July 8, 2007

Dawn Rainbow

A rainbow only bounces back to you the color in the light.
You get something quite special when the circumstance is right.
An early morning shower when the sun had hardly shown,
Caused the rainbow to get dressed in haste, in colors not its own.

Full golden was the rainbow, with neon at the edge,
As the sun was rising sleepily from beyond its earthen ledge.
I had never seen a rainbow that was monochrome like that,
But I remember vividly just where I was and where it sat.

There was no gold to find down on the ground beneath the bow,
For all of it was utilized in putting forth the glow.
No doubt you think I'm daft to even say I saw the sight,
For no one else has ever seen a rainbow in dawn's light.

Bobby G. Wells . . . . June 14, 2004

Discomfort

The warming sun is sleeping late,
The chill of darkness lingers.
Without my cup to keep them warm,
I blow upon my fingers.

I stand out on the waiting spot,
Bus timing is a puzzle.
Of late the morning dew has grown,
Some white around its muzzle.

Some weeks ago I sought the shade,
As sunshine made me suffer.
Today the shade seeks me instead,
What warmth have I to offer?

The warning comes in by degrees,
Soon Winter rules the land.
Discomfort would be welcome when,
I take my life in hand.

I half expect in Spring they might,
Discover that my statue,
Is only some poor rigid fool,
Flash frozen in his a-choo!

Bobby G. Wells . . . . September 28, 2007

Dark of Night

If I dream, I dream of night.
A starless sky of hidden moons,
Crickets tune their instruments,
And katydids hum nocturnal tunes.

A lullaby called "Come Hither,"
A song to soothe a friend.
With silences of darkswept breeze,
In woodland without end.

My eyes are all reflections,
As ghostly lights may play,
On billowed gauzy curtains,
In windows as they sway.

The place I am is restfulness,
The place I seek is Home.
My head will not rest easy here,
And still I choose to roam.

Bobby G. Wells . . . 1/11/2007

Distance

Stand at the shoreline. Look to the sea,
Weapon in hand as you see Enemy.
A weapon bloodied on those you hold dear,
A thing that is useless for he is not near.

Distance protects him. Distance will harm.
He will have distance from God's loving arm.
In cold outer darkness his soul will shrink down,
For God's loving smile has turned into a frown.

This one a failure. This one has flaws.
This one has broken the primest of laws.
And so cast away with no more than a glance,
The only true victim in his game of chance.

We see only shadows 'til light fills our soul,
And then we perceive what was always our role,
Of things in the Universe God may perceive,
Some items He'll treasure, and some He'll just leave.

We'll go on with Him to a Future of Light,
And distance will sunder what's left in the night.
Our future is golden, as friends gather round,
And no thought is given for what is cast down.

Bobby G.Wells . . . . December 9, 2005

Down on the Road

My wife's cat got killed down on the road the other day,
Expending all of its lives in a futile, final moment.
Probably, it's better that it happened quickly,
We wouldn't want the beast to live in torment.

We never got around to giving it a name,
Translating just as friendly sounds,
And we were just some folks it saw,
In making its appointed rounds.

The necessary burial detail fell to me,
I've had too much of practice in the task.
I'd just as soon it fall to someone else,
To let me shrug and wonder if she'd ask.

"So, have you seen the cat of late?
The poor thing must be ready to come round …"
"No, Dear. I haven't seen it,
It's probably in another part of town."

The comfort of not knowing would be welcome.
Instead I have the dread of knowing truth;
That cats will go a-hurrying across a road,
As if the hounds of Hell pursueth.

Cats and highway vehicles don't mix too well,
The feline wiring won't admit,
That there are times and circumstances,
When cat-quick reflexes don't fit.

And thus the grisly task inherits me.
Holding back my tears with stoic face,
I perform a silent duty to a former friend,
Caught between a wheel and a hard place.

Then walking back to put away the shovel,
I have a little time to give it thought.
Please let someone do the same for me,
When I have lost the final battle that I fought.

Just put me down where frost won't make me shiver,
And cover with a blanket made of grass,
Amidst the roots which always smell so pleasant,
Of soda-scented sweetened sassafras.

Bobby G. Wells . . . March 19, 2008

Doohickey

Netherness, and otherness, and oneness are nice,
But commonly commonness will often suffice,
To do what is needed, and function quite well,
And still be attractive, with a story to tell.

I've seen situations, where a doohickey's gone,
And a suitable substitute is then seized upon.
Like an old rusty tractor, when the lever's not right,
Where some vice-grip pliers may have plied their last bite.

They have welded themselves, through tenacity's glue,
And they've served just as well as a doohickey'd do.

Bobby G. Wells . . . . June 22, 2007

Eyes Lift Up

In the collapse of those two towers,
Some saw a nation fall.
But what we lost was innocence,
They'll see we can stand tall.

We reached up once and touched the moon,
And showed the world a way,
That man could reach out for the stars,
And leave his feet of clay.

Some do not choose to rise with us,
They're bound so to the Earth,
They wish to make us fall down, too,
And let dreams die before their birth.

It may be that our feet are soft,
Our will is made of steel,
To those who love the dirt so much,
The command will ring out. Heel!

To balance out the lives we lost,
A new thing has been born,
We don't know where the path will end,
That started Tuesday morn.

Our striving is for upward,
The glow of Heaven calls,
Snares and stumbles will not stop us,
Nor will any of our falls.

The fall of towers, fall of men,
The fall of years we have to spend,
As long as life and love rise up,
We do not care where it will end.

Our gaze is fixed upon the stars,
With vision of a Heaven firm,
We'll lift ourselves as freedom soars,
And leave the dust to dreamless worm.

Bobby G. Wells . . . . . April 25, 2004

Faded Flags

There are a lot of faded flags. They've grown a tattered gray,
That were so bright and vibrant when we hung them on that day.
The fresh pain now has faded, and control is grimly kept.
The hurt that washed into our soul made furrows as we wept.

Faded too is memory, perhaps a blessed thing,
Except we get reminders of the terror that they bring.
They think they can deflect us. They hope they can prevail.
I have a bit of news for them, WE ARE NOT GOING TO FAIL.

We showed our children Peace and Love, they turned a little green,
And found compelling entertainment in a video machine.
We watched in horror as they chortled at the gore,
We hardly knew that they were hardening for War.

Our enemies underestimate the ease with which we cringe,
For they haven't seen our kids go on a video killing binge.
They are prepared for battle, all we need to say is go,
"Game over"'s when they'll note the scores belonging to the foe.

We didn't want them trained this way, but since it's come about,
I think we ought to let the kids just let their feelings out.
They'll vent a lot of anger, and we'll cheer them from the side,
And they'll sweep away the flaming horde just like a rising tide.

And faded colors of the flag will gain a brighter gleam,
As the new recruits are added to the old part of the team.
Some may return with wounds and mental hurt that keep them blue,
While others will be stellar in the things they have to do.

The purest of their valor will be shown within the fight,
And white will represent them in the dawn's approaching light.
And yes, we will have casualties. Many smiles will end up dead.
And we'll sew the bravest color in their shroud in brightest red.

Bobby G. Wells . . . . . . May 19, 2004

Flowers From The Garden

There is a window in your heart, that opens on a garden,
A place you can retreat to when you need to ask for pardon,
For having been abusive, to the child that lives in you,
By simply asking way too much, for any child to do.

Don't ask for the surrender, of childhood dreams so gay,
That they could always bring a smile, despite a rainy day.
The toys we had as children, were of the simplest sort,
A cardboard tube became a sword, a cardboard box a fort.

Children can be happy, they've learned the art of play,
Try not to lose that talent as you go about your day.
With all the noise and bustle that distracts you from that art,
Take time to smell the flowers from the garden in your heart.

Bobby G. Wells . . . . May 11, 2004

Flowers

I look at the soil of darkness and putrescence,
How can flowers find sustenance there?
And yet from soil and sunlight they somehow,
Will lift perfection in the air.

The honeybee enjoys the harvest,
And journeys deep in the flower-bell.
She wallows in the joy of life,
While we only get a smell.

Bobby G. Wells . . . March 28, 2005

Free Admission

I just get free admission to the show,
When talent is the coin that gets you,
Where you want to go,
I just get free admission to the show.

Well, some folks say I'm talented, and others that I'm blessed.
It isn't something special that I do,
I'm putting words together just like beads upon a string,
And when I'm done I show them all to you.

And that's what gets me in to see the show,
They must just think I know someone up high,
They always let me just go walking by,
So that I get free admission to the show.

They like to listen to me, and I like to make noise,
So that's the way to play the game for me.
Sometimes they gather round me when I'm gathered to myself,
And sometimes I'm alone as I can be.

And I just get free admission to the show,
I'm allowed to have free passage almost everywhere I go,
Cause someone thinks I'm special, but just how I do not know,
But I still get free admission to the show.

I wear smiles because I'm happy, and I never mind the pain,
It just runs right off my shoulders when it lands,
I'm as happy as a duck that has been caught out in the rain,
For my pain's no more than time upon my hands.

For I'm allowed admission to the show,
There's a blessing in each raincloud,
That's a truth I've come to know,
Cause I get free admission to the show.

I just get free admission to the show,
When talent is the coin that gets you,
Where you want to go,
I just get free admission to the show.

Bobby G. Wells . . . . December 26, 2005

Glory Bee

Out in the garden one sunny day,
A golden honeybee came buzzing my way.
She came straight to me, as if I,
Had nectar she might like to try.

I stared, entranced, as on she came,
And wondered idly what was her game.
And then she stung me! Holy Cow!
How come it wasn't hurting now?

Instead of pain, a glory spread,
Until I felt it in my head.
Her sting was not a strange attack,
But giving something that I lack.

Somehow she sensed a hole I had,
In spirit, and she made me glad.
It was an angel, Heaven sent,
To help me make my life content.

She's there in Heaven, with her wings,
And all those other angel things,
I'm sure a harp she couldn't do,
I guess she hums on her kazoo!

Bobby G. Wells . . . March 8, 2005

His Good Time

There's something rather inviting here,
If some work doesn't scare you away.
A lot of us think that running a farm,
Is just a big place we can play.

But the work begins before sunrise,
When the coffee is still not awake,
And it doesn't let off 'til you sit in the shade,
And sharpen your tools on your break.

Then you finish your work with the last fading rays,
And you put things away in the dark.
The sound of an "ouch" is the signal you've found,
That wheelbarrow you forgot to park.

I don't want to imply that there is no reward,
You can eat all you want that you've grown.
And there's nothing that adds to the flavor more,
Than to know it's from seeds that you've sown.

And you've watched your partner helping,
And you've thanked Him with all of your heart.
For He sent all the rain, and the sun in its time,
And you know that He's earned a big part.

It's ironic, you note from your window,
As He irrigates crops far and near.
You get your results by hard work every day,
While He takes His good time to appear.

Bobby G. Wells . . . . June 8, 2005

His Hand In Mine

When I was but a single cell,
My form had no design.
A shapeless mass without a plan,
God put His hand in mine.

I had no eyes or limbs,
How could I walk a line?
I did not know my fur from fin,
God put His hand in mine.

A guide to how my bones should grow,
A function quite divine,
A way to do the will of God,
God put His hand in mine.

So as I grew, I thought I should,
My soul to Him consign,
Where else was I to go but there?
God put His hand in mine.

At last my muscles and my bones,
Some purpose did define,
To do His work, with His own strength!
God put His hand in mine.

Some day, when I no longer may,
Work fruitfully as Thine,
Please guide me Home, my dearest Lord,
And put Thy hand in mine!

Bobby G. Wells . . . August 27, 2014

Waiting in the Wings

Their life, that is in you, listens.
Their life, that is in you, hears.
Your life may seem drowning in sorrows,
Their life, is beyond any tears.

His smile is a shining remembrance,
His touch will forever, hold.
His will is that you should continue,
As each of you grows to be old.

His visage will fade only slightly,
As wear and tear takes its toll.
His words you'll remember in fondness,
They'll be prompting the lines for your role.

Her words will be singing forever,
Her presence will seem to be near.
She will be guiding and smiling,
And helping your joy to appear.

The parted are not so departed,
You can feel their connection to you.
Remember the good ways you journeyed,
And remember the bad times were few.

Their life, that is in you, listens.
Their life, that is in you, hears.
They're waiting in wings for your solo,
And waiting to greet you with cheers.

Bobby G. Wells . . . . . May 24, 2004

What I Wanted To Be

What I wanted to be as a grownup,
Was a man, like my dad had once been,
He was faced with the challenge of living,
In a world where no thing was a sin.

He could have lolled in the barroom,
Getting drunk on the money he'd earned,
Instead of supporting a family.
He'd a choice, and the tempting was spurned.

In the rough circumstance of his township,
It was normal to act like a brute,
When your world is descending to chaos,
It's great fun to jump into the chute.

Instead, he scrabbled and struggled,
Against all the odds so arrayed,
Pushing all of us higher and higher,
While others just sat there and stayed.

They stayed where their fate had propelled them,
Like weeds growing up in a crack.
But Dad had a loftier goal for himself,
And the rest of us stuck on his back.

So, sure, it would have brought comfort,
And ease from the day's hurtful blows,
But a man like my Dad didn't care for that,
So he lifted his burden and rose.

With confidence in his ability,
And faith that the Lord would provide,
He clambered aloft from the place he'd been tossed,
With a woman as good by his side.

So these are the ones that I emulate,
You others may do as you choose,
I will climb till I've gotten above all the fray,
And I've shed all the things I can't use.

I've no room in my journey for hatred,
Or for jealousy making me weak.
I'm saving some room in my heart for the things,
That my trust in the Lord says to seek.

And strangely, the climbing gets easier,
As higher and higher we rise,
Somehow the goal seems much closer,
As its light finds its way to our eyes.

Bobby G. Wells . . . . . . June 14, 2008

The Fog

The fog came in so quietly, its purr was rather muted,
It seemed in such a playful mood. The sky was all transluted.
It shrouded all the buildings, and made their edges soft,
And silence filled up everything, until somebody coughed!

The mist absorbed the noise so made, as if so far away,
It could have been an echo from some sound another day.
The fog was curious, looking in, and checking every space,
And nose-to-nose, it rudely rose, and stared in every face!

Playfully, it glided round, and stalked its unseen prey.
And cotton-soft, it crept about, Night's Shadow into Day!
Then finally, a target found! As swiftly as could be,
It coalesced into a cloud, and gave a kiss to me!

Bobby G. Wells . . . . June 13, 2005

The Hours I Keep

My life is filled with treasures,
Rainbows, sunsets, lovely flowers,
Each I see as one more gift,
To set among my trove of hours.

Minutes stolen here and there,
Pondering the ways,
Glimpses of a bright tomorrow,
Mounting up to days.

Times I've taken stock of things,
Reckon I've done well.
Interest paid on gathered scents,
A fortune when I sell.

There will be an accounting,
Before my final sleep,
In minutes I've recorded for,
The hours that I keep.

Bobby G. Wells . . . . . May 21, 2007

Candle of Dreams

Draw out from the stone the cold fury of Earth,
Spin it into a fabric of power.
Wrap up your package of treasured things,
And be prepared for the hour.

Gather up all of the world about,
That you and your arms might hold,
Pile it as high as your wandering eye,
Can see with a clarity cold.

Prepare for the journey of only one step,
Prepare for baptisms of fire.
Rejecting the Earth is a dangerous game,
Your suitor's a world full of ire.

For all of these decades it's held you close,
That when now you should dare step away,
Watch out for a fateful hand reaching out,
To grasp and compel you to stay.

Ride fire and its anger up into the sky,
A guttering candle of dreams,
If all incantations have been muttered aright,
You'll rise on your magical beams.

Out there in the unwinking starlight,
The glare from your own is intense,
A scrutiny searing in scathing scorn,
For the dance you're about to commence.

We'll watch as you take your first flightsteps,
Man's reach must exceed his grasp,
That fate that all mortals are heir to,
Your world to its bosom will clasp.

And although you may have departed,
You're with us as we are with you,
For no one of us can be truly alone,
With the world keeping you in its view.

Bobby G. Wells . . . . September 1, 2008

The Last Goodbyes

Every time you say Goodbye, it is a last Goodbye,
And sometimes, it becomes a Last, without a hint of why.
I said Goodbye, some years ago, to a little girl of ten,
Just heard the news report today. I won't see her again.

It never should have happened. That much is always clear,
But accidents and tragedies don't care for time of year.
In Springtime, when the budding life is bursting out like song,
The loss of one so full of hope just makes the world seem wrong.

One never does expect it. Surprise is no surprise.
The Reaper dressed in party clothes is in a poor disguise.
Still I recall the time that I was last to see her leave,
I don't think it occurred to me I'd be the one who'd grieve.

We said Goodbye. It lasted long. A lifetime I suppose,
She should have gone about her life, for that is how it goes.
I wither and diminish. She flourishes and thrives.
But age is not the only thing that puts an end to lives.

Please take these notes in sadness, from lessons I have learned,
When you say Goodbye please make it Good,
and make the Last one earned.
Like Jefferson and Adams, each stricken to his bed,
Yet each was sure the other lived, on a day that each was dead.

Our Goodbyes have a purpose, they hold a memory,
A flash of frozen joyfulness, in case of tragedy.
Please make the most of them, and "photograph" the smile,
And hold that hug, or handshake. It has to Last a while.

Bobby G. Wells . . . . May 16, 2005

95

The Middle Distance

Off in the middle distance,
I often find my gaze,
While those who think I stare at them,
Don't understand my ways.

I give to them my neutral face,
And draw my mental shades.
My inner image overwrites,
And reality slowly fades.

My view is filled with diagrams,
Of circuits, graphs, and charts.
I don't intend the rudeness shown,
Such staring thus imparts.

I'm closed off in a world my own,
Your world has lost my focus.
If folks like me disturb your space,
Just reach across and poke us.

Bobby G. Wells . . . . . . August 29, 2007

The Inventor of the Bagpipe

His name was Cyrus Reedy,
And he'd been sent to Hell.
But Cyrus was a jolly sort,
And he just said, "Oh, well!"

"What's there for entertainment, then?
Ha'e ye perhaps, a band?"
And he paid no attention to,
His shrill demon's command.

He'd had a wife, he had, he had,
And she was wont to screech,
So by the time 'e got to Hell,
His ears were out of reach.

The demon's yells just made him laugh,
Until it lost its voice,
So Cyrus moved about with ease,
And roamed to suit his choice.

He found some stuff discarded round,
It gave the place its flavor,
But he was desperate for a sound,
That only he could savor.

He made up a contraption,
That made an awful wail,
The demons shunned him for the way,
Their ears he did assail.

He added bits and pieces,
The monster thing did grow,
And when he made the sound come out,
They said he had to go.

They threw him out of Hell, they did,
They couldn't stand the noise,
And that's why bagpipe music,
Is the kind that he enjoys.

Bobby G. Wells . . . . . November 14, 2006

The New Job

The curse of the Peter Principle,
Is that you rise too far,
Your meteoric path just marks,
The scene of a shooting star.

The burnout comes real quickly then,
And suddenly it's "splat",
Your hopes and aspirations,
Your dreams have fallen flat.

That's how it is for most of us,
Whose rise has topped the chart,
But some there are who need not fear,
This fate upon their part.

So modest when you meet them,
So capable and bright,
It's hard to see how anything,
Could be beyond their might.

With quiet understanding,
Intensity and joy,
When given challenges, they excel,
Each day begins, "Oh boy!"

They just keep moving upward,
With placid, stolid strides,
Excelling, with aplomb, you see,
And something else besides.

Just like a king or emperor,
They often speak of "we",
In challenges they've met alone,
They've had some company.

Sometimes they even speak as though,
Someone is at their side,
Someone to look up to,
And to speak at eventide.

"We thank You for the gifts You sent,"
He said, though quite alone.
"And for the talent You have lent,
We struggle to atone."

Bobby G. Wells . . . . October 12, 2007

A Difficult Season

This is a most difficult season. We've traveled a distance this year.
I'm growing increasingly worried. My dear wife and I are in fear.
Our journey has been quite a hard one, and
others have passed us in haste,
If we are to find some comfort, we haven't a moment to waste.

But she could give birth any minute. This motion is not a good thing.
We'll need to rest long when we get there, and
we'll need all the coin we can bring.
This traveling back to my hometown, means
that I and my child will share,
This place of birth and our kinship, with
others who dwell about there.

The town is decidedly crowded. There's not a room to be had.
The innkeeper lets us take shelter, in a stable nearby. It's not bad.
The earthy smells are a comfort, somewhat like a scent of new wood.
As a carpenter, I know I'll rest easy, if my
wife will agree that it's good.

I would think it could be a bit festive, with
a pine bough to sweeten the air,
And a candle or lamp, to keep out the night damp,
but I sit on the straw and just stare.
For beyond the smoke of our camp-fires, I
can see a bright star in the sky.
The heavens may have their works revealed,
but I cannot spare them my eye.

For my wife is finding comfort, in the straw of our rude little space,
And so, like it or not, I'm preparing, to
welcome our child in this place.
So a food trough becomes a first cradle, as
he comfortably makes it his own,
All swaddled about, with his face shining out,
he can reign like a king on his throne.

When I get to a place I can work at, I'll
make a good cradle, and sound.
A carpenter's son shouldn't have to accept, some
rough sticks in a bad part of town.

Bobby G. Wells . . . . . . December 16, 2008

A Home's Heart

The cabin grew small when the children arrived,
But the happiness fit, and the family thrived.
With a little more room when they added a part,
That surrounded the fireplace that is a home's heart.

With the breakfast in morning and smiles with the feed,
They scatter to fetch in the things that they need,
So when the day ends and they gather once more,
They'll be sharing some things you can't buy at a store.

There'll be laughter and stories, and some kids to be kissed,
And a song and a prayer, and some items I missed.
When the fire goes out, there's a sadness you sense,
That four walls without love ain't much more than a fence.

Bobby G. Wells . . . . April 11, 2005

Ante Up

Once the cards are shuffled,
And handed all around,
That is the hand you're dealt,
Whatever you have found.

You cannot have do-overs,
Where Life is what is done,
"This ain't exactly what I want,"
Just means you don't know fun.

It's not a game of aces,
Good cards at every turn,
But rather taking what you've got,
And applying what you learn.

Life has a way of making,
Good things from the mundane.
A busted flush can sometimes serve,
Who knows what you could gain?

Some think we're here to master,
A special kind of task.
And maybe what you need to learn,
May not be what you'd ask.

I'd like to be a rich man,
And live a life of ease.
But anyone can do that much,
From school days earning "D"s.

Accepting what you're getting,
With gratitude's a plus,
That's got to be the reason,
Why God puts up with us.

Bobby G. Wells . . . . . March 24, 2004

Bent Icicles

My house has bent icicles,
We've had some wind today,
It's like some ice-age carnivore,
That seeks to hold its prey.

Nature isn't nurturing,
That seeks to tear and rend.
Those icy fangs are scaring me.
It is a biting wind.

I'll venture out, quite soon I guess,
They don't scare me that much.
Even though they're growing longer,
And sharper to the touch.

I have something I have to do,
It seems compelling now.
I'm hoping later that I won't,
Regret it all somehow.

The imagery may seem quite bleak,
So stark in black and white.
It's warmer in the daylight though,
At least it isn't night.

And how much could it bother me?
I'm big and strong, and tough.
Those frigid fangs of winter,
Though dripping, are a bluff.

They cannot really hurt me,
It is a threat display.
I stand up straight and say these words,
"Can I stay home today?"

I have one thing consoling me,
When I walk out the door.
I'm not the sweetest person,
I'm salty at my core.

My warmth will not win me a friend,
Out in the frozen waste.
I've got this big, old ugly coat,
It will not like my taste.

I guess you wonder what it is,
I'm trekking out there for.
I found out that I'm running low,
There's birdseed at the store.

Bobby G. Wells 2/22/2004

Boy

They used to see my freckles when they looked at me,
And waves of curly hair upon my head.
My eyes would just be squinting out, below my knitted brows,
Some even thought my hair a shade of red.

Sun-bleached, I guess it was, because later it turned muddy brown,
And no one called me "carrot top" again.
I liked to think about the way things worked.
Deducing that I had a furnace in my skin.

It was right there in my belly, it rumbled so sometimes,
And its warmth was quite apparent, I can say.
However cold my hands became, my belly was still warmer,
Thanks to all the fuel I sent its way.

My mother always swore that I could grow potatoes,
In darkened furrows when I held my skinny elbows out..
I liked potatoes, but they never quite took root,
Erosion from the frequent storms of baths, no doubt.

I don't know about the other boys, but dirt was my companion,
My plaything for the little cars and men.
I built the roads they traveled on, and tunnels,
Road-building was less time-consuming then.

I still have marbles that I played with, then,
I haven't lost them all quite yet.
And hopscotch was another thing I did,
And I could probably beat you at it, I bet!

You'll notice I defined low maintenance,
Except for quantities of food and soap,
For clothing that I got from here and there,
And a corner where I hid to dream and hope.

I remember ice-cream that we worked to make,
And fevers that I sweated out at night,
My Dad's rough hands that rubbed my itchy back,
And always knowing things would be alright.

These things that I remember comfort me,
They gather round my thoughts at end of day,
But just like then I am not ready for my bed,
I'm still alive inside here, come and play!

Bobby G. Wells . . . . September 19, 2006

But Today

I'm worried about next week,
When some debts are coming due,
And concerns about my family's health,
Are constantly in view.

But today, the sun is shining,
And my heart is quite at peace,
For the moment, at this instance,
I'm not looking for surcease.

I have some years behind me,
And more yet still ahead,
But on the whole they pleased me,
More than filling me with dread.

For today, the birds spread wings of joy,
To embrace the world "this much",
Just as do I, in reaching out,
To keep my heart in touch.

In the distant future, when I as memory,
Will haunt the hills and hollows,
Of a changed vicinity,
Then my touch will be as follows:

Folk will be seeing rainbows,
Or singing birds in flight,
And sometimes thoughts of mine,
Will then intrude upon their sight.

For tomorrow will be coming,
While I wend another way,
And my focus will not be with things,
That may be coming, but today.

Bobby G. Wells . . . . . . March 1, 2008

The Crysalis

The butterfly and I share a secret,
We are secret agents of change.
Where each of us crawls into hiding,
To then let our souls rearrange.

That droll and tedious crawling,
The eating of leaves and such fare,
This isn't the fate we aspire to,
We're destined to soar in the air.

But somehow we have to make payment,
To store up the good things we dream,
In hopes that a last sleep will furnish,
The essence of all of our schemes.

So if you have not seen me lately,
It could be I'm taking a snooze,
In preparation for waking up,
And filling my eyes with new views.

Bobby G. Wells . . . . September 18, 2019

The Cotton Wagon

Oh, it is cool in the cotton shed,
When the sweat dries off, as you wipe your head.
Yes, this is where I would make my bed.
It's cool in the cotton shed.

Yes, and it's soft in the cotton piles,
Where we rest a bit, and restore our smiles.
I'd like to ride for miles and miles,
It's soft in the cotton piles.

My, it's good to relax when your work is done,
And to take relief from the heat of the sun,
Just resting is all that I need for fun.
It's good when your work is done.

But you can't stay long resting in the shade,
These wagons will head for a big parade,
For some pennies a pound that the farmers made.
No you can't rest long in the shade.

Bobby G. Wells . . . . May 7, 2005

Why Were My Hopes So Hidden?

Why were my hopes so hidden?
They seemed a quite normal kind.
I just wanted children and family,
And watching our lives unwind.

Something has happened to me,
What it was I just cannot say,
How it happened or who did what,
That hurt me on that day.

At first, it was acceptable,
I felt love, and they gave me care,
In time, I guess I realized,
I wasn't going anywhere.

And then, the days grew longer,
My visitor list grew short,
My diary held blank pages,
And that is my report.

It's also condemnation,
For how my life has drained,
Out through the vacant window,
Of my vista now constrained.

I could have gone to parties,
With many a birthday chance,
I would have smiled at a party,
Even though I couldn't dance.

So why were my hopes so painful,
To those who had starred in my dreams?
I've shrunken to life in a bird-cage,
Even that's not enough for some schemes.

They debate about life that's worth living,
But they don't put their own lives in hock.
I'm inclined to believe that a just review,
Would have placed most of them into shock.

For the scales of true justice will measure,
The worth of those judging me,
And the hopes that I had that I treasure,
Far outshine any others I see.

Bobby G. Wells . . . . . December 10, 2006

When Bobby Was Seven

When Bobby was seven,
He liked playing games,
Liked working out puzzles,
And had puzzled aims.

He mostly was smiling,
About average size,
And his exercise program,
Involved mainly his eyes.

He liked to hear music,
Couldn't figure out dance,
His movements reflected,
All those ants in his pants.

As his friends fondly noted,
There was surely a way,
Having made it to seven,
He'd grow up one day.

Bobby G. Wells . . . 27 Feb,   2015

I Only Want ...

I only want a million days,
To loll around and squander,
And idly, in a drunkard's path,
About the hills to wander.

A million days of sunrise,
Begetting jeweled morn,
And sultry softened afternoons,
With rain no hint to warn.

The rain may fall in eventide,
To lull a resting soul,
As smiling for the joy of life,
Relinquishes control.

Such perfect days are metered,
We get so very few,
A million such seem adequate,
If one has aught to do.

I'd intersperse them with a touch,
Of raw days and of storm,
Which wouldn't count among the list,
Just give excuse to warm,

While waiting out the frozen count,
Of days on which I feed,
Before the fire of stored delight,
Preserved for such a need.

Bobby G. Wells . . . . May 17, 2008

As Long As I Live

In one of my first adventures,
I traveled as a fox,
I then became a cat or two,
(I think outside the box!)

Of course, back in my caveman days,
So much I did not know!
The warm inviting firelight,
The cold, warmth-drinking snow.

As Robin Hood, my Merry Men,
Could entertain me well,
In hidden bowers of the wood,
Where I and they did dwell.

I didn't like the dying,
But that's a part of life.
You take the bitter and the sweet,
And struggle with the strife,

For this is why you're living,
Here in the folded lands,
The flat landscape that opens up,
Uncovered by your hands.

Transferring wisdom through those funnels,
You call eyes into your head,
To give you memories of past lives,
As gifts of what you've read.

For now the thousand lives I've led,
Inure me to some pain,
Those joyous friends I will not see,
Unless I read again,

Yet still they wait, on dusty shelves,
For other eyes than mine,
Like goblets for the next to taste,
Their own first sips of wine.

Bobby G. Wells . . . . . June 26, 2008

Only Fourteen Years

I'm looking at my Calendar, and ET's looking back,
Way back in 1983 that fella had a knack.
He didn't need a band-aid, or other medicine,
Just held a glowing finger up, and up zipped up the skin.

Fingers are salutes for us, this year just as back then,
And purple is the in thing now, to dip your finger in.
But back to this strange alien, and why he's here with me,
And why I'm looking at some dates from Nineteen Eighty-Three.

That year began on Saturday, just like the current one,
And it was not a leap year, so when all is said and done,
The calendar I have in hand will serve me well this year,
For every date will line right up, as each month does appear.

For there are only seven ways to start the New Year's play,
And only on the leap years do you need that extra day,
So fourteen calendars are quite enough, no matter how you age,
Just shove the old one in a drawer, and don't mark up the page.

I know the Nation's printers will be annoyed I've made it known,
That you don't need to purchase what you already own,
But think of all the Playmates who can give that happy smile,
Now that they realize they won't grow old for quite a while.

Bobby G. Wells . . . . February 8, 2005

Show Me More!

Show me more! Show me more!
I don't want to be there yet.
For the things that I have seen so far,
I never will forget.

Let me see, let me be,
Let me look out through the glass,
A wondrous fascination comes,
With every thing we pass!

I have loved, I have touched,
I have hugged the world *this* much!
It's been like a candy playland,
Filled with milkshake dreams and such!

Show me more! Show me more!
Do not make me old too soon.
I want to see the people out there,
Dancing on the moon!

Tell me shush, tell me hush,
Tell me I have been long blessed,
Then tell me there'll be more to see,
After just a little rest.

Bobby G. Wells . . . . . . February 6, 2008

Reflections

God sets a mirror down for us,
To bounce back sunny days,
He does it when the rain has passed,
To help us see the rays.

The reflection that we see in it,
Is not of hair and skin.
What we see is an image of,
The gloried state we're in.

Light pink, and brighter orange,
And yellow brighter still.
I sit and look at glory's frame,
Upon my favorite hill.

The others call it rainbow,
But I know what it is,
A magic mirror in the sky,
That lets us know we're His.

The body that we occupy down here,
Is nothing like its start,
For one, the most attractive thing,
Has always been the heart.

God looks into our heart and then,
Just for His own amusement.
He gives a glimpse of what He sees,
And laughs at our confusement.

"That doesn't look at all like me!"
I hear your protests start,
But when you look at other folks,
How can you see their heart?

If you admit there's beauty,
Reflecting from some source,
Just think how glorious it will be,
When He's revealed full force.

And you and I are with Him,
And joining in the glow.
Next time you see a rainbow,
I thought you ought to know.

Bobby G. Wells . . . . April 5, 2004